THE SCRIPTURES, THE CROSS AND THE POWER OF GOD

THE SCRIPTURES, THE CROSS AND THE POWER OF GOD

N. T. Wright

Bishop of Durham

First published in Great Britain in 2005

Society for Promoting Christian Knowledge
36 Causton Street
London SW1P 4ST

British Library Cataloguing-in-Publication Data
A catalogue record for this book is available from the British Library

ISBN 0-281-05770-2

1 3 5 7 9 10 8 6 4 2

Typeset by Graphicraft Ltd., Hong Kong
Printed in Great Britain by
Bookmarque Ltd

for Michael Sadgrove

Contents

Contents

Preface

———◆◆———

In Holy Week 2005 the Dean and Chapter of Durham
Cathedral invited me to give the addresses which would
carry the week from its dramatic opening on Palm
Sunday to its solemn and glorious conclusion on Good
Friday and Easter Day itself. This allowed me to work
through familiar material in a fresh way, within a context of prayer, liturgy and worship in one of the greatest buildings of the Christian world. This little book
reproduces, with a minimum of re-editing, the nine
addresses I gave during those eight days.

The services at which I spoke began with Mattins
on Palm Sunday. Since the reading that morning was
Matthew's version of the parable of the Wicked Tenants
(21.33–46), and since Matthew (like Mark and Luke
but in his own way) uses that story and the following
material to interpret Palm Sunday on the one hand and
look ahead to Good Friday and Easter on the other, I
decided that for the next three days, speaking at the
evening service of Compline, I would explore the stories
in Matthew 22 in the same way, showing how they
carry forward and develop the densely integrated themes
at the heart of Jesus' ministry and its extraordinary
denouement. Then, on Maundy Thursday morning, we
had a service of a different sort, at which most of the
diocesan clergy were present to reaffirm their ordination vows, and at which we consecrated the oils which,
in obedience to the scriptural command in James 5.14,

were to be used in ministry. I took the opportunity there to expound Matthew 23.1–12 from the same point of view.

On the evening of Maundy Thursday we commemorated, at the Eucharist, the footwashing scene in John 13.21–32. That gave me the opportunity to switch tracks to John's interpretation of the events leading up to Jesus' death, and I continued with John when preaching at the main Good Friday service. Having followed Matthew and John thus far, I was then able to preach on their two accounts of Easter Morning, first at the early morning vigil, at which I baptized and confirmed several candidates, and then at the main Easter service at the Cathedral.

I took as my subtext, throughout the week, the comment which Jesus made to the Sadducees: that they were wrong because 'they knew neither the scriptures nor the power of God'. Both Matthew and John understand the events of Jesus' last week as the climax of the entire biblical narrative, and as the great moment when God's power – made known, paradoxically, in the human weakness of Jesus himself – was unveiled for the rescue and remaking of the world. I made no attempt to articulate a full theological account of the meaning of the cross, either for Matthew or John, or for Jesus himself, or as one might re-express it for today. There is an enormous amount that could be added. But I hope that these addresses, by approaching the question from less familiar angles, will contribute both to the enriched understanding, and also to the empowered living out, of the vital and inexhaustible events at the heart of Christian faith.

Preface

The translations at the head of each passage are taken from my beginning-level guides to the New Testament, the Everyone series (in this case, obviously, *Matthew for Everyone* and *John for Everyone*, both published by SPCK in 2002 and by Westminster John Knox Press in 2004). The poem quoted near the start of the final address is my own, taken from the opening chorus of *Easter Oratorio*, whose music is by Paul Spicer.

One of my great joys at being Bishop of Durham has been the chance to work closely with one of my oldest friends, the Very Reverend Michael Sadgrove, now Dean of Durham. His warm support and encouragement came into fresh focus during Holy Week 2005. My dedication of this book to him is a small expression of my deep gratitude and affection.

N. T. Wright
Auckland Castle

1

PALM SUNDAY
MATTINS

The son and the stone
(Matthew 21.33–46)

———◆◆◆———

'Listen to another parable,' Jesus went on. 'Once upon a time there was a householder who planted a vineyard, built a wall for it, dug out a wine-press in it, and built a tower. Then he let it out to tenant farmers and went away on a journey.

'When harvest time arrived, he sent his slaves to the farmers to collect his produce. The farmers seized his slaves; they beat one, killed another, and stoned another. Again he sent other slaves, more than before, and they treated them in the same way. Finally he sent his son to them.

'"They'll respect my son," he said.

'But the farmers saw the son.

'"This fellow's the heir!" they said to themselves.

"Come on, let's kill him, and then we can take over the property!"

'So they seized him, threw him out of the vineyard, and killed him.

'Now then: when the vineyard-owner returns, what will he do to those farmers?'

'He'll kill them brutally, the wretches!' they said. 'And he'll lease the vineyard to other farmers who'll give him the produce at the right time.'

'Did you never read what the Bible says?' said Jesus to them:

The stone the builders threw away
Is now atop the corner;

It's from the Lord, all this, they say
And we looked on in wonder.

'So let me tell you this: God's kingdom is going to be taken away from you and given to a nation that will produce the goods. Anyone who falls on this stone will be smashed to pieces, and anyone it falls on will be crushed.'

When the chief priests and the Pharisees heard his parables, they knew he was talking about them. They tried to arrest him, but they were afraid of the crowds, who regarded him as a prophet.

If a visitor from Mars – or even, perhaps, from some remote South Sea Island – had been in Cardiff on the Saturday before Palm Sunday 2005, they could be forgiven for being puzzled. The entire city was in an uproar over an event which took less than two hours, which involved a lot of frantic running around on the part of thirty people and a lot of shouting on the part of tens of thousands. When it was all over, there was wild jubilation for many, and misery for the rest.

And if we were to explain to the Martian visitor just why the Welsh rugby victory over Ireland was so significant, we would have to tell a story. We would talk about the days of old, the great days when one tiny country could take on the world. We would talk about the long years in between, years of hoping and waiting and trying again and again. And we would talk of the gathering excitement over the last three months, as the faint dream started to become possible, the possible suddenly looked likely, and the likely only had two hours between it and certainty. And it is that long story, accompanied no doubt by a lot of puzzled head-shaking from our visitor, that would explain the day-long uproar in the city.

The uproar in Jerusalem on the first Palm Sunday has a similar explanation, which sets the context both for this morning's reading and for the sequence of readings and reflections that we shall be following over the next few days. We shall only understand what was going on if we think of a people with memories considerably longer than those of Welsh rugby fans: memories kept fresh by regular tellings of ancient stories and regular re-enactments, in ritual and festival, of what had happened in times past and what would, they hoped, happen again in the future, this time decisively and for ever. They were stories of King David coming to Jerusalem and taking it, making it his capital and the centre of a surprising kingdom that, under himself and his son Solomon, ruled over all its neighbours and lived in freedom, peace and prosperity, the brief envy of the ancient Near East. They were stories of that kingdom being divided, of Jerusalem being attacked, of brave kings like Hezekiah and Josiah who cleansed the Temple and kept the foreign armies at bay. They were stories of disaster and exile, of shame and destruction, and the prophetic hope for a rebuilding and renewal when YHWH himself, Israel's God, would come to the rescue. And, much more recently, a mere two hundred years before Palm Sunday itself, they were tales of a small devoted band, Judas Maccabaeus and his followers, who had recaptured Jerusalem and the Temple after the Syrians had desecrated it, who came into the city waving palm branches to celebrate the divine victory over the hated enemy, who cleansed the Temple to be again the place of YHWH's holy presence, and who thereby established a royal dynasty that ruled for a hundred years. Those were the stories – that was the great Story – which had sustained them for many generations, and at last they really believed that the stories were coming true, that the great Story was reaching its climax.

And Matthew, like all the gospels – but it is Matthew we shall be following in this chapter and the ones that come next – is saying, in his own telling of the story of Jesus, what Jesus himself was saying over and over again throughout his ministry. It's true: the great Story is indeed reaching its climax; but the ending is not what you had expected. They had expected a warrior king, and Jesus came riding on a donkey, speaking of the way of peace. They had expected someone who would restore the Temple fully and finally, and Jesus came with an acted parable of its destruction. They had expected a son of David who would drive out the pagan enemies and leave Israel mistress of the nations, and Jesus came speaking of a son of God who would be rejected and killed, but who would turn out to be the Stone, the corner-stone of God's new building. I have tried to think of what the parallel to such an overturning of expectations might be in the world of my opening illustration, but it's hard to do so. Maybe we could catch the flavour of it if we said that the Welsh rugby team, having run out onto the field, were, instead of playing rugby, to acquire stringed instruments and play a long, slow, Celtic lament before the astonished crowds.

The Palm Sunday story which Matthew tells, alongside Mark and Luke, then naturally leads into a sequence of parables and disputes in which Jesus confronts the chief priests, the elders, the Sadducees, the Pharisees and the crowds in general. It's all too easy for us, with a kind of semi-familiarity with this material, to forget what job they are doing in the overall story, but the evangelists never forget it: these short scenes are meant, on the one hand, to explain what Jesus' action in the Temple was all about, and, on the other hand, to explain in advance what his next actions would mean. What Jesus did in the Temple on Palm Sunday and what he did in the Upper Room on Maundy Thursday go together as a pair of mutually interpretative actions, and together they point of course beyond themselves to the greatest action of them all, the one which follows on Good Friday. And my purpose in this chapter and those that immediately follow will be to explore Matthew's sequence of parables and disputes in such a way as to bring out that flavour, so that these are not detached stories but contribute to leading our blind eyes up to that horrifying moment of utter truth and to opening our anxious hearts to the message it contains.

When we see it like this, today's parable of the vineyard and the wicked tenants, of the father, the servants and the son, comes suddenly into sharp focus. In one of the later disputes, Jesus rebukes his hearers because they don't know the scriptures or the power of God; and this story might have been told with the same underlying moral. Jesus is reworking the poem we find in Isaiah 5, the story of a vineyard and its owner and of the vineyard's refusal to bear the proper sort of grapes. Everyone knew what this meant; Jesus didn't need to say at the end, 'if you have ears, then hear', because everyone had heard and they knew what he was talking about. He has expanded Isaiah's poem so that now the problem is not with the vineyard itself but with the tenants, in other words, the present rulers, actual and

6

self-appointed, of God's people. This, in fact, is one of
the main themes of all the discourses, of the Palm Sunday action itself, and of the terrifying final discourse
which follows, predicting the ultimate destruction of
city, Temple and all. The problem upon which Jesus
has turned the spotlight, the problem which they didn't
want to acknowledge and which we don't want to
acknowledge, so that Palm Sunday is always in danger
of collapsing into sentimental kitsch with its donkey
and its palm branches – the problem is that evil isn't
something 'out there', it's something which has infected
all of us, God's people included; so that if we knew our
business we would turn all the more quickly from shouting 'Hosanna' to praying for mercy.

For them, within Jesus' parable, they had had plenty
of warnings; the vineyard owner had sent messengers,
his servants the prophets, and they had been beaten,
killed and stoned. Now he has sent the son; and, seized
with envy, they have grabbed him, thrown him out of
the vineyard and killed him. This parable is one of the
most explicit statements anywhere on Jesus' lips of his
own unique status as one doing the job of a prophet
but himself being far more than a prophet, of his own
unique role as the one after whom the father has no
one else he can send, and of his own unique and shocking vocation to bear in himself the hostility and violence of those to whom he has been sent. There is as yet
no atonement theology in this parable, except insofar
as the parable makes it plain, with its echoes of the
scriptures and its evocation of the power of God, that
somehow this violent death will itself be part of the
plan, the plan not to tell everyone that everything is all
right after all but to come to the heart of the place

where it's all wrong and to allow the full force of that wrongness to be worked out, hammered out, in his own body. Somehow, the parable is saying, things must all go horribly wrong in order that things ultimately may be put to rights. The son of God will come himself to the place where evil is doing its worst, even when that place is not out there in the pagan world but in here within the people of God, and take its violent fury upon himself.

Only then can the other saying come to pass, that the stone which the builders rejected is to become the cornerstone. The Hebrew words for 'stone' and 'son' are very similar – *eben* and *ben* – so that the saying about the stone and the parable about the son are meant to work together, both with the warning of terrifying judgment and with the promise that God will fulfil his purposes, will bring in his kingdom, will vindicate his people over against the forces of evil. But the people who are to be vindicated are the people whose identity is for a moment hidden within the Stone, the Son – hidden because the people who thought they were God's people have turned out to be keeping the vineyard for their own ends, and can't stand the thought that the owner might send his own son to stop their play-acting and require the fruit which was rightfully his.

Much of Holy Week consists, or ought to consist, in our going back in mind and heart to those first and unique events. In our day particularly we need to be reminded that what happened then was not just one example of a general pattern, but the central and un-repeatable events which form the hinge upon which the great door of cosmic history has swung open at last. That is perhaps the hardest thing for our generation to believe, and we have to rub our noses in it over and over again. But when we do that – when we grasp the unique and decisive and one-off nature of those events, from Palm Sunday to Good Friday and on to Easter itself – we discover again, and it's bound to be almost as deeply disturbing, that there are similar lessons always to be learnt in the church and in our own hearts and lives. When Jesus comes to his church, and to his people, today, he comes with the same message, and with the same warning. He comes seeking fruit, the fruit which belongs to his father. And those of us who decide to make the journey from Palm Sunday to Good Friday can never therefore do so in anything other than fear and trembling. We are, says St Paul, the temples of the living God. God forbid that when the Lord whom we seek comes once again to his temple he should find it necessary once more to come with stories of judgment. May we so hear the word, so live within the story, that we find ourselves in six days' time at the foot of the cross, and in eight days at the empty tomb, and find ourselves saying, 'This was the Lord's doing, and it is marvellous in our eyes.'

2

MONDAY OF HOLY WEEK

The king and the guests
(Matthew 22.1–14)

———◆◆◆———

Jesus spoke to them once again in parables.

'The kingdom of heaven', he said, 'is like a king who made a wedding feast for his son. He sent his slaves to call the invited guests to the wedding, and they didn't want to come.

'Again he sent other slaves, with these instructions: "Say to the guests, Look! I've got my dinner ready; my bulls and fatted calves have been killed; everything is prepared. Come to the wedding!"

'But they didn't take any notice. They went off, one to his own farm, another to see to his business. The others laid hands on his slaves, abused them and killed them. (The king was angry, and sent his soldiers to destroy those murderers and burn down their city.) Then he said to his slaves, "The wedding is ready, but the guests didn't deserve it. So go to the roads leading out of town, and invite everyone you find to the wedding." The slaves went off into the streets and rounded up everyone they found, bad and good alike. And the wedding was filled with partygoers.

'But when the king came in to look at the guests, he saw there a man who wasn't wearing a wedding suit.

' "My friend," he said to him, "how did you get in here without a wedding suit?" And he was speechless. Then the king said to the servants, "Tie him up, hands and feet, and throw him into the darkness outside, where people weep and grind their teeth."

'Many are called, you see, but few are chosen.'

The story of the king's great supper breaks several of the little moulds with which we have often domesticated the shocking message of Holy Week, and indeed of Jesus and the kingdom of God in general. For a start, we have to scrap the old distinction between parable and allegory: Matthew tells us that Jesus is here speaking in parables, but almost every line shouts out 'allegory!', applying both to Jesus' ministry in general and to the specific themes we find elsewhere between Palm Sunday and Good Friday. As with the preceding parable of the Wicked Tenants, the son in the story is clearly Jesus himself, and the king, like the vineyard owner, is obviously God the father. The main point of Jesus' self-reference as 'son', however, is not in the first instance a trinitarian hint (though we shall have that before the week is out), but an increasingly clear claim that Jesus is the Messiah, the son of David who, in the Old Testament and later Jewish writings, is spoken of as God's adopted son.

Another mould to be broken here is the idea that Jesus only ever said the same thing once, so that similar stories or parables must be parallel developments from a single original – in this case the stories of a dinner party in Luke and in the so-called *Gospel of Thomas*. That theory has enabled many writers in the last two or three generations to sigh with relief and ascribe the terrifying last four verses to Matthew rather than Jesus; we'll get back to that in a moment. The point here is partly that good, pithy parables and allegories are much harder to construct than you might think – even the rabbinic parallels are flat and mundane by comparison, and it would be surprising if Matthew or Luke possessed a talent for composition comparable to that of

Jesus rather than to that of their Jewish contemporaries – and partly of course that Jesus, as a wandering teacher in the days before mass media, naturally said similar things over and over again, no doubt developing them this way and that as he went along. Our present story thus draws both on folk tales known in the culture and on other things Jesus had said often enough before, though this time with a new kaleidoscopic twist in the tail.

One more broken shibboleth is the idea that there was an ancient Jewish belief in a coming messianic wedding feast. Actually, tonight's passage has a good claim to be the first time the idea appears. Before this we do indeed find a messianic *banquet*; but only here, then in the parable of the Ten Girls three chapters later, and then in Revelation 19, has this become an actual *wedding* feast. The bride, and except for the opening mention the bridegroom too, are absent in this story, but like characters in a Beckett play we should perhaps be aware of them none the less.

All this leads us to the first main point Matthew has in mind, which is that this story is a further explanation of what Jesus had done in the Temple on Palm Sunday. How so?

Like the wicked tenants, who reject the messengers, including finally the son, and so court disaster, so the invited but ungrateful guests, in an obviously allegorical line, seize, beat and kill the messengers who are summoning them to the wedding reception. Like the vineyard owner punishing the tenants, the king sends troops to destroy the city where the wedding guests apparently live. Both parables indicate what we should have known anyway: that what Jesus did in the Temple

14

was an acted parable of judgment. Like Jeremiah smashing his pot, Jesus was prophetically saying that God would overturn not only the money-tables but the very stones with which the Temple was built. The present sequence of teaching, of course, leads the eye up to Matthew 24, where this is made as explicit as apocalyptic language can get.

This is where we, like the Sadducees later on, need to be reminded again of the scriptures and the power of God. We are not talking about how God acts in relation to isolated individuals in any culture and at any time. We are talking about the dark but God-driven climax of the scriptural narrative. The coming messianic banquet was the fulfilment of all the hopes of Israel, the time when YHWH would put everything to rights, the time when the purpose for which God had called Israel in the first place would at last be accomplished. The whole point of there being a chosen people was that through them the creator God would heal the ancient wrongs of the world. So when the prophets summoned Israel to fresh obedience it was in order that God's purpose in election might go ahead. And when Israel seized, beat and killed the prophets, a theme which comes again and again in the present chapters, such actions could only be seen as a fierce rejection of election itself, a rejection which would lead at last to the final prophet symbolically declaring that the whole point of there being a holy city, a Jerusalem, a Temple, a sacrificial system, was now a thing of the past, and that God was about to fulfil the same plan by a more focused and frightening route.

And that would lead, of course, to the rejection of the prophet himself. The underlying question posed by

Jesus' Temple action, the question which rumbles on underneath these chapters until it surfaces like a volcano when Jesus stands before the high priest, is: Who does Jesus think he is? Only one person has the authority to act in the Temple in the way he had done – only one person, that is, other than the high priest himself. It was David who planned the Temple, Solomon who built it, Hezekiah and Josiah who had cleansed it, Zerubbabel who had rebuilt it, Judas who had cleansed it again, Herod who was rebuilding it. Destroying and rebuilding the Temple was an inescapably royal thing to do. Jesus' saying about destroying and rebuilding, which had gone round the rumour-mill several times by now, was (and everyone knew it was) a veiled claim to royalty. It is the son of David who declares the Temple redundant, and who thereby draws on to himself the divine purposes for which the Temple had stood as a thousand-year advance symbol. The father has indeed prepared a marriage feast for his son, and the feast will indeed take place. But the city of those who refused the invitation will be burnt with fire.

What then will follow? Somehow, God's purpose will go ahead anyway. The choice of Israel wasn't a mistake, but the purposes God intended to carry out through Israel are now to be carried forward by the son, alone. The building of the Temple wasn't a mistake, but now the place of sacrifice will be the son, alone. The mystery at the heart of the parable is the mystery at the heart of the gospel itself: that all alike have refused the father's call, and that the son, who is himself the final rejected messenger, will take that rejection itself and turn it into the means whereby the father's purpose will finally be accomplished. But that is to run slightly ahead of ourselves. What about the central theme of the parable, the one which is partly so obvious to us and partly so opaque?

The central theme is the sudden lavish throwing open of the invitation no longer to the great and good but to all and sundry. Everyone found in the streets is to be invited to the banquet. We sigh with relief. Jesus is playing our tune at last. Here is the gospel we know and love, the message of a radical inclusivity in which the doors are thrown open for all to come in. And it's true, and it's glorious, and it needs saying again and again.

But the point at which we can tell that we are only hearing the bits of the message that we want to hear is the point where the story twists round and we confront a reality so unwelcome, so out of tune with the spirit of our age, that we move quickly to shut Matthew up, like the grown-ups shushing the child at the table who blurts out the truth the nice guests weren't meant to hear. What about the man without the wedding robe? What about the weeping and gnashing of teeth?

This is where we meet the same point as at the end of John's story of the woman taken in adultery. How easy it is for us to gloss over the last line. What we want to hear is the word of forgiveness: 'No more do I condemn you.' What we would rather *not* hear is the necessary word that follows: 'Go, and don't sin again.' As in the Sermon on the Mount, the great blessings on all and sundry at the beginning are matched by the stark warnings at the end: some will say 'Lord, Lord', but the Lord will not recognize them. As in the parables in Matthew 13, the 'good and bad' are kept together for the moment, but ultimately separated out. Because, of course, without the warnings, grace is subverted into

17

mere tolerance. One of the great moral and spiritual fault lines of our time lies just here. Paul puts his finger on it in Romans 6.1: if God acts in lavish grace to utter sinners, wouldn't it be best to go on being utter sinners so that we can get more grace? Paul's answer – Matthew's answer – Jesus' answer – is quite simple. *Mē genoito*. Let it not be. Many are called; few are chosen.

And the 'few', of course – this, too, seems to be part of Matthew's point, and it leads to my own final one – are in the process of being narrowed down to a single person. This is the twist within the twist in the tail of the parable. This is how the story does indeed, like all the stories of Holy Week, lead the eye strangely from Jesus' action in the Temple to the actions that follow on Maundy Thursday and Good Friday. The wedding banquet takes place, but the principal food on offer is the body and blood of the bridegroom. The king passes sentence on the unready guests, and the one who suffers the penalty is the king's own son. One man is indeed stripped of his garments, bound, or rather nailed, hand and foot, and cast out into outer darkness, and again it turns out to be the king's son, the bridegroom himself. The invitation does indeed go out to all, but it is the summons to stand at the foot of the cross. As the story unfolds, the dream of the wedding feast becomes first a bad dream, then a nightmare.

And it is that nightmare, the terror we call Good Friday, that breaks all the remaining moulds into which we had poured the gospel of Jesus to make it safer and easier. This is why we not only need the parables and stories of Matthew 21 and 22 to help us get from Palm Sunday to Good Friday, but we also need Palm Sunday and Good Friday to help us understand the parables and the stories. The scriptures and the power of God come rushing together in the person of God's Messiah, only to go tumbling with him, down, down into the dark, bottomless pit of sorrow and shame. And only when we have stood aghast for three days on the edge of that pit will we be in any fit condition to speak once more of the wedding banquet, of the lavish welcome, of the new Temple, of robes of true holiness, and of hope. Only when we have pondered what it cost the king to prepare the wedding banquet of his son dare we once more call God father and pray for the coming of his kingdom.

3

TUESDAY OF
HOLY WEEK

The tribute and the resurrection
(Matthew 22.15–33)

———♦•♦———

Then the Pharisees went and plotted how they might trap him into saying the wrong thing. They sent their followers to him, with the Herodians.

'Teacher,' they said, 'we know that you are truthful, and that you teach God's way truthfully. You don't care what anyone thinks about you, because you don't try to flatter people or favour them. So tell us what you think. Is it lawful to pay tribute to Caesar, or not?'

Jesus knew their evil intentions.

'Why are you trying to trick me, you hypocrites?' he said. 'Show me the tribute coin.' They brought him a dinar.

'This . . . image,' said Jesus, 'and this . . . inscription. Who do they belong to?'

'Caesar,' they said.

'Well then,' said Jesus, 'you'd better give Caesar what belongs to Caesar! And – give God what belongs to God!'

When they heard that they were astonished. They left him and went away.

The same day some Sadducees came to him. (The Sadducees deny the resurrection.) Their question was this.

'Teacher,' they began, 'Moses said, "If a man dies without children, his brother should marry his widow and raise up seed for his brother." Well now, there were seven brothers living among us. The first got married, and then died, and since he didn't have children he left his wife to his brother. The same thing happened with the second and the third, and so on with all seven. Last of all the woman died. So: in the resurrection, whose wife will she be, of all the seven? All of them had married her, after all.'

This was Jesus' answer to them:

'You are quite mistaken,' he said, 'because you don't know your Bibles or God's power. In the resurrection, you see, people don't marry or get married off; they are like angels in heaven. But as for the resurrection of the dead, did you never read what was said to you by God, in these words: "I am the God of Abraham, and the God of Isaac, and the God of Jacob"? He isn't God of the dead, but of the living.'

The crowds heard this, and they were astonished at his teaching.

Holy Week is framed within the crash of coins. Money all over the floor on Palm Sunday as Jesus overturns the tables. Thirty pieces of silver flung down by Judas on Friday. Poised between the two, Jesus examines one small coin, small as a sixpence, powerful as an eagle. Money, and its political meaning, is central to Holy Week.

Similarly, resurrection. Jesus tells the disciples on the road that he will be crucified, and raised three days later. As usual, they haven't a clue what he's talking about; but it happens. And here, halfway between, we have the Sadducees challenging Jesus about the resurrection. That, too, is central to Holy Week.

It may seem odd to lump these two trick questions together. Matthew and Luke follow Mark in placing them back to back at the heart of the string of stories which link, and which help us to interpret, Palm

Sunday on the one hand and Good Friday on the other. The question about tribute to Caesar is not, in other words, simply a question about (what we call) 'church and state', or 'religion and politics'. The Sadducees' strange question about the woman with seven husbands (and Jesus' almost equally strange answer) is not simply a detached story to show what Jesus believed about the resurrection. The Caesar-question and the Sadducee-question form a further double explanation of the cleansing of the Temple and the meaning of the Passion.

This is where Jesus utters the rebuke which I have made thematic for this book: you are wrong, he says, because you don't know the scriptures or the power of God. This doesn't just apply to the Sadducees' denial of the resurrection. Though Jesus doesn't quote the scriptures in his response about Caesar's coin, he is appealing implicitly to the entire scriptural narrative about God's people living under pagan rule, a line of thought from Exodus to Judges to Isaiah and Jeremiah and, supremely, to Daniel. His point is precisely that the very way his interrogators have asked their question about paying tax to Caesar shows that they have forgotten this scriptural line of thought, and the power of God – and the kingdom of God, ruling over all pagan power – to which it bears witness. The key to understanding this passage is to realize that, seen from within the scriptures and in the light of the power of God, money is also a theological issue, and resurrection is also a political issue. Together they take us towards the heart of Holy Week.

When Jesus was still a boy, thousands of Jews were crucified for refusing to take part in Rome's census and the consequent taxation. The anti-taxation movement was led by a man named Judas. His slogan was the one Jesus would later adopt: the kingdom of God. Calling yourself a God's-kingdom person then must have sounded like calling yourself a Fifth-Monarchy man in the seventeenth century, or a Jacobite in the eighteenth – and, perhaps like them, you would also be evoking the scriptures and the power of God. That's why the Pharisees, the scripture-based hardliners, tended to oppose the tax and support the revolt.

And it was precisely among those revolutionary groups that belief in resurrection was flourishing. Resurrection wasn't a pretty way of talking about life after death. It was a way of talking about a new bodily life *after* 'life after death', about God putting everything back to rights, raising all the righteous dead to share in the new this-worldly kingdom of justice and peace. People who believe that God is doing that, and that they will be part of it – as opposed to people who believe that God will destroy the present world and take them off to a spiritual 'heaven' – are very likely, in the name of that God and the hope of that future, to work for God's justice here and now in advance. Resurrection is a political issue. That's why the Sadducees, the rich conservative aristocracy, opposed it tooth and nail.

So the question of the tax, and the question of resurrection, go to the heart of the real underlying question: what did Jesus think he was up to on Palm Sunday, and where was it all leading? If Jesus was announcing God's kingdom, acting in the Temple as if he thought he were the Messiah, with the right to declare the Temple itself redundant, was he then backing the anti-tax, anti-Caesar movement? Was he backing the resurrection-movement, the let's-put-the-world-to-rights movement? Could he be smoked out into making some kind of a statement which would condemn him either in the eyes of the Romans, for being an ordinary revolutionary, or in the eyes of the hardliners, for not really meaning what he said about God becoming king?

Fresh in the folk memory behind the movements of Jesus' day stood the glorious revolution of another Judas, Judas Maccabaeus. It was he who had entered Jerusalem with palm branches waving, cleansed the Temple and founded a royal dynasty. Maccabaean echoes haunt this pair of stories.

First, 'render unto Caesar'. Mattathias, the father of Judas Maccabaeus, had zealously defended the holiness of God, the Temple and the law. His last words to his sons were: 'Pay back the Gentiles what they deserve, and give attention to the command of the Law.' Render to the pagans, in other words, what belongs to the pagans, and to God what belongs to God. And he wasn't telling them to pay the tax. He wasn't giving them a guideline on the separation of church and state. Paying back the pagans as they deserved – in other words, revolution – was part of their duty to God.

But Jesus was looking at a coin. His questioners had begun with a piece of flattery which doesn't translate well into English: you don't defer to anyone, you don't regard people with partiality. Literally in Greek, following the Hebrew idiom, the latter phrase is 'you don't look at people's faces'. Now here he stands confronting a small but perfectly formed face, that of Tiberius Caesar, and around the face are the words, 'Tiberius Caesar, son of God, Son of the Divine Augustus'. And on the reverse, an image of the goddess Pax, peace, with the words *Pontifex Maximus,* High Priest. You get the message? Look at the face, pay the tax, and the son of God, the true high priest, will give you peace. It's the proud boast, *mutatis mutandis,* of every empire, ancient and modern. Imperial tax is a theological issue: feel the crackling tension as the son of God, the image of the father, the true high priest, confronts the image of the proud pagan who claimed the same titles. 'Pay Caesar back what belongs to Caesar, and pay God back what belongs to God.'

Roll back the layers of meaning and see what Jesus has done. He has quoted, more or less, a revolutionary slogan. But with Caesar's coin in front of him he points simultaneously to a different truth, a different kind of revolution. Rome could have no authority unless it had been given from above, as he says to Pilate. The powers that be are not divine, despite what they imagine, but they are ordained by God, and must be *both* respected *and* held to account by God's people. That is the ancient Jewish view of pagan authorities, and the question is then open in any particular instance to say, what does 'respect' involve in this case, and more particularly, what does 'holding them to account' involve in this case?

With that question we see at last the wider connection with the theme that runs from before Palm Sunday through to Good Friday. How does Jesus call the powers to account? Not by the normal means of kingdom-inspired revolution. James and John, on the way to Jerusalem, asked for the best seats in the kingdom. No, says Jesus: the rulers of the Gentiles lord it over them, but it won't be like that among you. Whoever wants to be great among you must be your servant, just

27

as the son of man came not to be served but to serve, and to give his life a ransom for many. The whole story of Jesus going to the cross is a political story, a story about the critique and redefinition of political power. It is *within* that story that we find the theology of the kingdom of God, the theology of atonement, and within that again that we find the meaning of the cross for ourselves today. Caesar had said, throughout Jesus' lifetime, pay the tax and have my 'peace', or I'll crucify you. And Jesus, with the money thrown to the floor, pays Caesar what he demands in blood instead, while with the same act giving to the father what he had asked, the servant-obedience through which the powers of the world are confronted with the power of God.

It is that power, of course, which then answers the question of the Sadducees. Their story, too, has a Maccabaean ring: their tale of seven brothers and a wife echoes strangely the story in 2 Maccabees of seven brothers and a mother who go to their martyrdom proclaiming that God will give them their bodies back in the resurrection. But Jesus is redefining resurrection even as he affirms it. Note that he doesn't say that the dead will *become* angels in heaven. They will be *like* them – in this respect: when they have been raised to a new immortal bodily life, they will not need to propagate and hence to marry. In other words, the resurrection will involve not a simple resuscitation to the same kind of life as before, but transformation into a new mode of bodily life. And in the meantime, before the resurrection of all the righteous dead, they are safe and well and alive in the presence of God, as is strongly implied by God's word to Moses about his being the

God of Abraham, the God of Isaac and the God of Jacob.

A different kind of resurrection; a different kind of revolution. When God announced himself to Moses as the God of Abraham, Isaac and Jacob, the immediate context was Israel's slavery in Egypt, and the immediate meaning was: I am about to fulfil my promises and set my people free. Resurrection and liberation go hand in hand. The scriptures and the power of God: God will indeed act again to rescue his people from their bondage and slavery. That is the meaning of Easter, the moment when, so Matthew tells us, Jesus is set in complete authority over both heaven and earth.

Put the Caesar-question and the Sadducee-question back together, and what do we find? We find Jesus, on the way to the cross, drawing together upon himself the great evils of the world, the imperial systems with their financial demands, and the great hopes of the world, hopes for God to release the slaves, to raise the dead, to set the world to rights. The scriptures give us the grounding for this hope; the power of God assures us that it will come. That message provides both the deeply personal meaning of Holy Week for each one of us and the deeply political meaning for today in a world that still groans under the slavery of the empire's financial demands. But the way to the resurrection is precisely through death, the death which Caesar demands as the price for declaring a different empire, the death through which Jesus offers to God that which is God's, his own life, his own obedience, his own Image.

4

WEDNESDAY OF HOLY WEEK

The Law and the Lord
(Matthew 22.34–46)

———◆◆◆———

When the Pharisees heard that Jesus had silenced the Sadducees, they got together in a group. One of them, a lawyer, put him on the spot with this question.

'Teacher,' he said, 'which is the most important commandment in the law?'

'You must love the Lord your God', replied Jesus, 'with all your heart, with all your life, and with all your strength. This is the first commandment, and it's the one that really matters. The second is similar, and it's this: You must love your neighbour as yourself. The entire law consists of footnotes to these two commandments – and that goes for the prophets, too.'

While the Pharisees were gathered there, Jesus asked them,

'What's your view of the Messiah? Whose son is he?'

'David's,' they said to him.

'So how then', said Jesus, 'can David (speaking by the spirit) call him "Master", when he says,

> The Master says to my Master,
> Sit here at my right hand,
> Until I place your enemies
> Down beneath your feet.

'If David calls him "Master", how can he be his son?'

Nobody was able to answer him a single word. From that day on nobody dared ask him anything.

The Pharisees' question to Jesus, and his to them, form the final pair of short dialogues in Matthew 22 and its parallels, the sequence which takes us forwards from Palm Sunday, which it explains, to Good Friday, towards which it looks. Once again we are face to face, in Jesus' actions and teaching, with the scriptures and the power of God: the scriptures, to which Jesus goes back repeatedly, since he believed they were reaching their climax in him; the power of God, not confined to the glory of heaven but, in Jesus, bringing God's kingdom on earth as in heaven. The pain and the promise of that is what Holy Week is all about.

Not, of course, that you'd know it from the media. On the Good Friday of the week in which this book was born I glanced to see what was on television. There was a re-run of a documentary about Pontius Pilate on the History Channel; there was good old Zeffirelli on BBC3; but on our five main public stations, apart from a short piece in the morning, there was nothing to indicate that this wasn't just another ordinary day. For anyone looking for the coming together of heaven and earth, the best they could have found would be two films: *All Dogs Go to Heaven* on Granada, and *Daleks – Invasion Earth* on Channel 4. That says it all, really.

But heaven and earth, and their coming together, are what Holy Week is all about. One of the hardest theological lessons for us is that when ancient Jews said 'heaven', they didn't mean a place far off up in the sky. They meant God's sphere of reality, the place where God lives, and where his future purposes are kept in store. 'Heaven' isn't a purely future entity. It is God's sphere, as 'earth' is ours. And the point is that God's sphere and ours *intersect*. They overlap, they interlock, sometimes they even merge. This is the foundation of all sacramental theology (a theme for another time).

If you'd asked a first-century Jew where heaven and earth met, they would have said at once, 'The Temple'. Read the Psalms and see. 'God is in the midst of her, therefore she shall not be moved.' And if you'd said, supposing you can't get to the Temple, how can you get to the same result? they would have said, 'The Torah'. Keep Torah and it's like being in the Temple.

So what does it mean that on Palm Sunday Jesus acted out a dramatic symbol of the Temple's destruction? What does it mean that he spoke of it being destroyed and also rebuilt – a saying which, no doubt garbled, was repeated against him at his trial? What does this mean not just about the Temple but about the coming together of heaven and earth?

At first sight the two dialogues we read seem to have little to do with these questions. The first is a question about the greatest commandment in Torah, with Jesus' response about love of God and neighbour. The second is Jesus' own question: how can the Messiah be the *son* of David when David himself calls him 'Lord'? But on closer inspection these two dialogues have everything to say about the question of heaven and earth, the question of the Temple, and the meaning of the strange events that come rushing upon us in the next four days.

It is Mark who, unusually, makes the point explicitly in relation to the first dialogue. When Jesus gives the answer that loving God and neighbour draws together the whole Torah, a listening scribe comments: 'You are right, teacher; because if you love God like that, and your neighbour as yourself, that is worth more than the entire sacrificial system.' In other words, Torah, like Temple, is a place where heaven and earth intersect; and if you've fulfilled Torah completely, you won't need the Temple. Precisely, responds Jesus. You've got the point. You're not far from God's kingdom. That's what Palm Sunday is all about.

Why? Because the long aim of Jesus' ministry, of bringing God's kingdom on earth as in heaven, includes what you might call the re-humanization of human beings, the sign of which is that love for God which formed the central command to Israel ('Hear, O Israel, the Lord our God, the Lord is One, and you shall love the Lord your God . . .') and that love for one another through which a new community comes into being. But we are sinful and selfish creatures; how can the wounds of our unloving natures be healed? How can our sins be dealt with so that we can be as God wants us to be, especially if the Temple is taken away? As we find elsewhere in the gospel story, Jesus has a cure for hardness of heart, a cure which has bypassed the Temple altogether. But to understand it we have to move to the second of the dialogues.

This time Jesus takes the initiative. Having seen off his questioners, he now asks them a question they can't answer. Everybody knows that the Messiah is the son of David. That was a loaded point, because everybody also knew that the present kings of the Jews, the house of Herod, had no connection whatever with David. But Jesus isn't pressing that. He is urging them to search the scriptures, to consider the power of God, and to probe more deeply into who exactly the Messiah might be.

Psalm 110 speaks in glowing terms of what Israel's God will say to the coming king. But David the

Psalmist doesn't say, 'YHWH says to my *son*', but rather, 'YHWH says to my *Lord*, Sit at my right hand, until I put your enemies under your feet.' What's going on? And what does it mean that the Messiah will sit at YHWH's right hand?

The short answer, and with it the vital connection between Palm Sunday, Good Friday, and indeed Easter Day itself, is that *Jesus is now the place where heaven and earth meet*. His own unfathomably rich vocation, his own intimate knowledge of the one he called 'Abba, Father', his own sense that he was called to do, solo, what in the scriptures only Israel's God gets to do, namely, to rescue Israel and the world from evil – all of this comes together in his own fresh reading of Psalm 110, his discovery, at the heart of his *messianic* vocation, of an element which no other would-be Messiah seems to have tapped into at all: that the Messiah is to be David's *Lord*, not simply David's son.

This is not a denial of Davidic sonship. Matthew could hardly have suggested that, after all he's said earlier in the gospel. Jesus is saying that hidden *within* the vocation to be Messiah was the vocation to be the one who would sit at the right hand of the Majesty on high, Lord of David, Lord of the whole world. It was by combining Psalm 110 with Daniel 7.13 ('the son of man coming on the clouds') that Jesus gave his final answer to Caiaphas at the night hearing, the answer *both* to the question about destroying and rebuilding the Temple *and* to the question about Jesus' identity, the answer that led directly to the charge of blasphemy and the sentence of death. Jesus is indeed the Messiah, and his prophecy about the Temple's destruction will indeed come true. And he will be vindicated, exalted to the place spoken of in the Psalm, the place at the right hand of the living God, sharing the throne of God himself. He, not the Temple, is the place where heaven and earth meet.

This claim, in fact, goes exactly with the implicit claim behind the messianic statement of Palm Sunday. As they got near Jerusalem, Jesus told a story about a king going away, leaving his servants with tasks to perform, and then coming back to see what they'd done. It isn't a story about Jesus going away and leaving the church with things to do; it's a story about God leaving Israel with a task to perform, and then coming back at last, as promised by the prophets. When Jesus came to Jerusalem that last time he was conscious of the vocation to embody, to incarnate, the return of YHWH to Zion. Knowing the scriptures and the power of God, he was rooted in those texts which spoke of the Messiah precisely as the one who would share God's throne; and he combined them with those texts which spoke of the Messiah suffering and being vindicated. The Messiah is David's Lord, not simply David's son; and the irony is that the claim for which Jesus was condemned was the very claim which he interpreted in terms of his vocation to bear in himself the ultimate suffering of his people.

The saying about David's Lord and David's son thus propels us back to the question about the great commandment. Not a jot or tittle, said Jesus in the Sermon on the Mount, will pass from Torah until all is accomplished; and as he articulates the greatest commandment in Torah, so he is on the way to its ultimate accomplishment. The vertical commandment, that we should love God with all our heart, is joined together with the horizontal commandment, that we should love our neighbours as ourselves; and Jesus combines the vertical and the horizontal into the greatest symbol of triumphant love the world has ever seen, a symbol at once clear and obvious and yet fathomless in its profundity, all the more so for its having been up to that point a symbol of the triumph of Caesar, his coins and his empire. The cross stretches up to God in loving obedience, and out to the world in loving service, and all because it is not only David's son but David's Lord who hangs there, so that the real stretching out is downwards, from God to us.

The cross of Jesus Christ is thus the ultimate place where, at last, heaven and earth meet and are reconciled. The Temple is redundant because the reality to which it pointed – the meeting of heaven and earth, and the sacrifice which is the gift of heaven to earth and the worship of earth for heaven – has now been clothed in flesh and blood. That is why Easter, when it comes, is the true beginning of the new creation, the new heavens and the new earth embodied for ever in the person of David's son, David's Lord.

And that is why love is the greatest commandment; because love is the mode of knowing appropriate for ultimate reality. When, in the eighteenth century and since, Western culture split heaven and earth apart and imagined a great gulf between them, it not only enshrined a profoundly non-Jewish and non-Christian world-view at the heart of our society, it invented modes of knowing to match: an ultimate split between 'objective' knowing of 'facts' and 'subjective' awareness of 'feelings' or 'experiences'. Our culture has oscillated between those two ever since. But the point about love is that love affirms the truth and the otherness of the Other while simultaneously delighting in it, producing a single 'knowing' which embraces objective and subjective and transcends both.

It isn't the case, then, that love just happens to be top of the list in a collection of arbitrary ethical imperatives. Love is the key that unlocks the inner being of the cosmos. It is the centre of Torah because Torah itself, like the Temple itself, was the place where heaven and earth met, as they now meet climactically and for ever in Jesus and his cross. As Wittgenstein said, it is love that believes the resurrection; and, we might add, it is love that stands in faith at the foot of the cross. As we go forward to the Upper Room, where all the stories and symbols of Holy Week converge, and thence to Calvary and Holy Saturday, to wait in silence for new creation to be born, we are sustained, even in the darkness, by the love, the fully accomplished Torah, of the one we know as David's son and David's Lord.

5

MAUNDY THURSDAY MORNING

Humbled and exalted
(Matthew 23.1–12)

———— ◆◆◆ ————

Then Jesus spoke to the crowds and to his disciples:

'The scribes and Pharisees', he said, 'sit on the seat of Moses. So you must do whatever they tell you, and keep it, but don't do the things they do. You see, they *talk* but they don't *do*. They tie up heavy bundles which are difficult to carry, and they dump them on people's shoulders – but they themselves aren't prepared to lift a little finger to move them!

'Everything they do is for show, to be seen by people. Yes, they make their prayer-boxes large and their prayer-tassels long, and they love the chief places at dinners, the main seats in the synagogues, the greetings in the market-places, and having people call them "Rabbi".

'You mustn't be called "Rabbi". You have one teacher, and you are all one family. And you shouldn't call anyone "father" on earth, because you have one father, in heaven. Nor should you be called "teacher", because you have one teacher, the Messiah.

'The greatest among you should be your servant. People who make themselves great will be humbled; and people who humble themselves will become great.'

'You have one instructor, the Messiah; and the greatest among you will be your servant.' These words link our gospel reading with a seminal passage three chapters earlier, the passage in which Jesus rebukes James and John. In a world where many are asking the question of

42

whether religion and politics can sit comfortably side by side, we discover not for the first time that the gospel story is inseparably political as well as theological, and that its challenge comes uncomfortably close to home, not least in Holy Week and particularly on Maundy Thursday.

Think back to James and John on the road, wanting to sit at Jesus' right and left in the kingdom; and remember Jesus' rebuke to them: it is pagan rulers who lord it over their subjects, but it mustn't be like that with you. With you, whoever wants to be great must be your servant; because the son of man didn't come to be served but to serve, and to give his life a ransom for many. That astonishing upside-down claim, replete with what we call political meaning as well as what we call theological meaning, serves as a heading for the whole story of Holy Week, a major theme for Good Friday itself, and a searching, disturbing question for those clergy who meet together on Maundy Thursday to renew, and I trust to reflect afresh upon, the promises they have made to God and to one another. We are called to be part of the upside-down community, or rather the right-way-up community, living out that painful and costly putting of the world to rights which took place in the great events we shall be commemorating and celebrating over the next three days.

So when, in today's gospel, Jesus turns the spotlight on the pressure groups who have cornered the market in the Jewish orthodoxy of his day, we need to get down inside what he's saying. The scribes and Pharisees play roughly the same role within first-century Judaism that the media play in our world, taking a high moral line on anything they like and denouncing those who fail to keep up to it, binding (in other words) heavy burdens, hard to bear, and putting them on other people's shoulders, while not themselves lifting a finger to move them. Of course, not all journalists are like that, but today's media give plenty of people the chance to pontificate at a distance, safe in the knowledge that their own lives are unlikely to be held up to the same scrutiny they enjoy imposing on others.

But it would of course be wrong, today in particular, for us to play the same game by pontificating safely about the media themselves. In the same way, it would be wrong to follow so many scholars in the last generation who have shrunk back in horror from the harsh words of Matthew 23 and have been only too eager to suggest that they come from Matthew himself, writing a generation after Jesus. This passage goes too closely with the Sermon on the Mount, and (as I said) with Jesus' earlier rebuke to James and John, for us to wish it away so easily. It offers a desperately uncomfortable challenge not only to the world, but to the church, and particularly to ourselves who represent the church and its message in the public eye.

The first message from this passage is that of *integrity*. The Pharisees, says Jesus, do not practise what they teach; but you must. Because we live in a world of words, of public pronouncements, of press releases and media spin, it is all too easy to suppose that because we know what words to *say* in the pulpit or in the counselling room, in an article for a parish magazine or the local newspaper, that we are somehow automatically good at *doing* them ourselves. Though we do not in our tradition take care about our phylacteries or fringes (the tassels that hang down below the coat and show how

44

devout an orthodox Jew really is), we have, dare I say, our own local equivalents.

And we cannot, alas, think that we have solved the problem by simply following another part of our contemporary culture and doing away with robes and formalities altogether. When I read Jesus' warnings about those who love the best seats in the synagogue, I don't instantly think of the rather unobtrusive clerical stalls to right and left of a chancel. I think, today, of the kind of worship where two or three people appear on stage, like a rock group, facing the congregation and dictating, as their mood directs, their every thought and prayer. Of course there are equivalents in every tradition, but my point is that we have not solved the problem by changing the outward formalities. Indeed, my own preference for the unobtrusive side-on leading of worship can itself pass very quickly into thanking God for the superiority of my own tradition: O Lord, I thank thee that I am not proud and arrogant like other worship leaders. Pride at one's own humility is one of the last hiding-places of the tempter – and it comes all too easily to those who, for social, cultural or psychological reasons, incline naturally towards inverted snobbery, which is simply another form of pride.

The key point remains: Integrity. The world is quick, now, to spot it when it's not there; indeed, the same newspapers that shout loudly that religion should have no place in our public life take delight, whenever they can, in exposing corruption in the church, as a way of saying, 'There you are! Told you so! They're all hypocrites really.' And that, in a postmodern world, is perhaps the greatest challenge to us who sign on and make promises before God and the world, promises to be faithful stewards of Christ's mysteries. Supposing you stay, as some clergy have stayed, in one parish for ten years, for twenty, or even for thirty. Actually people will have got the measure of you after three or four; but the challenge is to live in such a way from the very first day that people will know that when you speak you speak with a conviction that rings true right across your whole life. That is why we expect, indeed require from one another in public ministry, the highest standards across the board. There is simply no place in the ministry of God's church before the watching world for people who want to play God's game one day and the world's game the next. It is our life, as well as our teaching, which must say to the increasingly pagan world all around what Jesus said to James and John: the pagan world runs things one way, but you must do it the other way.

From integrity, then, to *humility*. 'All who exalt themselves will be humbled, and all who humble themselves will be exalted.' We can, no doubt, spot all too easily the first-order application of this. Those of us who wear dramatic clothes in church and stand up at the front and have a lot to say can easily imagine that this makes us important. Fortunately, our Lord in his mercy has a habit of sending a sufficient number of thorns in the flesh to keep us humble, but that itself implies that we need keeping humble, and will need it as long as we are in this body. We should perhaps, on a regular basis – and if Maundy Thursday isn't a good day for spring-cleaning, when is? – read Matthew 23 carefully and prayerfully and ponder our current practices and styles. We are not, says Jesus, to be called rabbi, or teacher, or father, or instructor. Well, we've developed ways of getting round half of that, just as we've developed ways of avoiding what Jesus says about money. And of course from the very beginning there were different offices in the church: apostles, prophets, pastors, evangelists, teachers and so on. There must be some way of signalling the church's recognition of our different gifts within the body of Christ. But they are precisely within the body of *Christ* – of the Messiah who humbled himself and became obedient unto death, even the death of the cross.

Part of our difficulty here is that 'servant ministry' and 'servant leadership' were all the rage just a few years ago. We sang 'The Servant King' until we were blue in the face. And now, if we're not careful, we find ourselves singing that extraordinary song – it's hardly a hymn, since it's addressed to one another, not to God – which could only have been written by someone in danger of death by introspection: 'pray that I may have the grace to let you be my servant too'. The relentless self-examination by which one might discover whether one really had the grace to let someone else be one's own servant is, I fear, exactly that kind of self-absorption from which the gospel of Jesus Christ ought to set us free. Part of genuine humility is to get up, shake oneself out of convoluted navel-gazing, and get on cheerfully with the work we've been given.

Because the point of integrity and humility is precisely not that they are the qualities we need if we are to feel pleased with ourselves. The point of integrity and humility is that they are the sign to the watching world that Jesus, not Caesar, is Lord. *And there has seldom been a time in our national and international life when we have needed to say that more than we do right now*. Churches in the Western world are beginning to find a voice within public debate, though not always in ways we might have expected.

The newspapers scream, of course, that only fundamentalists would try to bring religion into politics; in other words, please don't disturb our nice secular worldview. But the whole point of Jesus' warning to James and John, the warning which echoes in Matthew 23, the warning which stands right across Holy Week and leads us to the very foot of the cross, is just this: the pagan rulers do it one way, but you must do it the other way. Read Isaiah 40—55, and watch the way the development of the picture of the Suffering Servant through those chapters matches, stride for stride, the development of the political critique of pagan empire. 'Draw near, you survivors of the nations – they have no knowledge, those who carry their wooden idols, and keep on praying to a god that cannot save. Turn to *me* and be saved, all the ends of the earth, for I am God, and there is no other. To me, and me alone, every knee shall bow, every tongue shall swear.' And Paul declares in Philippians that it is to *Jesus* alone that every knee shall bow and every tongue swear.

That is the challenge to the pagan world: the irrepressible news that there is a God who calls the world to account, and that this God is revealed fully and finally in the Servant, in the Jesus who was obedient to the death of the cross. The reason we must always be testing our patterns and habits of thought and action, we who bear public office within the church, is not so that we can feel smug and humbler-than-thou, but because we are charged with the urgent task of calling the world to account before the Servant King, of reminding the world that there is a God and that his power is made

perfect in weakness, of saying to the rulers of this age
that the true Lord of earth as well as heaven is the Jesus
whom we follow and serve. And in that task our principal weapons, alongside faith, hope and love and the
word of God, are the integrity and humility for the lack
of which Jesus indicted the scribes and Pharisees.

And so we come, not simply to a renewal of vows,
not simply to a consecration of oil for its various purposes, important though those are, but to something
so familiar and yet always strange; because this meal
always calls us to fresh contemplation of the utter integrity and humility of our Lord himself. Think, as you
take the bread and drink the wine, of these simple gifts
precisely as the embodiment of that integrity and
humility; chew them, drink them down, let yourselves
be formed and transformed by them; go out with that
integrity and humility to proclaim Christ crucified and
risen this Good Friday and Easter; and do so with power
and boldness before the powers of this world who still
keep praying to gods who cannot save.

6

MAUNDY THURSDAY
EVENING

Betrayal and glory
(John 13.21–32)

After saying this, Jesus was troubled in his spirit. He told them why.

'I'm telling you the solemn truth,' he said. 'One of you will betray me.'

The disciples looked at each other in shock, wondering who he could be talking about. One of the disciples, the one Jesus specially loved, was reclining at table close beside him. Simon Peter motioned to him to ask who it was he was talking about. So, leaning as he was very close beside Jesus, he asked him, 'Who is it, Master?'

'It's the one I'm going to give this piece of bread to', said Jesus, 'when I've dipped it in the dish.'

So he dipped the piece of bread, and gave it to Judas, son of Simon Iscariot. After the bread, the satan entered into him.

'Do it quickly, won't you?' said Jesus to him.

None of the others at the table knew what he meant. Because Judas kept the common purse, some were thinking that he meant, 'Buy what we need for the festival', or that he was to give something to the poor.

So when Judas had taken the bread, he went out at once. It was night.

When Judas had gone out, Jesus began to speak.

'Now the son of man is glorified!' he said. 'Now God is glorified in him! And if God is glorified in him, God will glorify him in himself, and glorify him at once.'

'The one who ate my bread', quoted Jesus at the table, 'has lifted his heel against me.' This is the point in the story at which the scriptures and the power of God come together in the way which fulfils Jesus' own words about humility and exaltation: because the betrayal of one of Jesus' closest associates indicates more clearly than anything else could do the strange truth that God's power is made perfect in weakness.

We were reflecting in the last chapter that love is the mode of knowing appropriate for the new creation. This is dramatically underscored here in John 13, where Maundy Thursday takes its name from the new commandment, the new *mandatum*, that Jesus' followers should love one another as he has loved them. That will be the sign that they are indeed his disciples. Only shared allegiance to him can draw together such a disparate collection of people.

But this foregrounding of love has as its corollary the fact that this knowledge is always deeply vulnerable. Love can be taken advantage of. Love can be betrayed. If it can't, it isn't love. That is the price and the preciousness of love. We ought therefore not to be surprised that one of Jesus' followers cracked under pressure.

It is strange (I say this in passing, but it becomes relevant) that we refer to him as Judas, the Greek form of the name, when the name is of course identical to that of the patriarch Judah, Jesus' own ancestor, and for that matter the same name as one of Jesus' brothers, perhaps the author of the letter of Judas (Greek), Judah (Hebrew) or Jude (obscure, but apparently English). Judah, *Yehudah* in full Hebrew, means 'praise'; and in the heroic Jewish legends of Jesus' day it was of course a revolutionary name, borne by Judah the Maccabee two centuries before and Judah the Galilean two decades before. Perhaps . . . but perhaps we shouldn't speculate. I was going to say that perhaps the Judah who betrayed Jesus had thought that maybe if they killed Jesus they would need someone else to lead the kingdom-movement; perhaps someone with a name both royal and revolutionary . . .

But the main point is that though for us the name 'Judas' sticks out like a sore thumb (and did so already when, very soon after Easter, people were telling the stories and giving lists of the Twelve, and dumping Judas at the end), if we called him 'Judah' he would simply be yet another to bear the royal name, the heroic name. They were a bit short on boys' names in first-century Judaism. In the index to Josephus, to look no further than the Js, there are 21 people called Jesus, 18 called Joseph, 11 called John, 15 called Jonathan, and 15 called Judas. In other words, Judas didn't stand out. He was one of the team. When Jesus said, 'One of you will betray me,' they didn't all turn round with a knowing, self-righteous look and say, 'Ah, that'll be Judas.' They all said, 'Lord, is it I?'

The story of the Supper, and not least the foot-washing, is thus a sign precisely of the vulnerability of love; of the love which, as we have followed through the story from Palm Sunday to this moment, we have increasingly come to recognize as the incarnate love of God. Everything in the Supper points forwards to Calvary, providing interlocking grids of explanation and interpretation for Jesus' death, not to domesticate it or contain it within a formula but rather after the manner of people standing at various places and all pointing, though shading their eyes against the glare, towards the dazzling event which they have glimpsed. It is one of the most important features of the whole story of Holy Week that, when Jesus wanted to give his followers the most accurate understanding possible of what he was about to do, he didn't give them a theory, he gave them an action: a meal, a Passover meal, a meal which was itself further interpreted by the footwashing.

First, a meal. A moment of friendship, of family. Love at table. The climax of all those meals, those parties, celebrating God's kingdom in Galilee. How strange, the night before an execution! And yet how right: because Jesus' death will defeat the power of evil once and for all, and so establish God's kingdom in a new way, a way from which all can benefit the way you benefit from a good meal. Jesus' death, the great act of love, will provide, at last, the messianic banquet to which all are invited.

Second, a Passover meal. The moment of liberation: the lamb, the unleavened bread, judgment on Egypt, the crossing of the Red Sea. One of the great things about our modern Easter celebrations is that we still retain the Passover imagery which Jesus himself chose as the interpretative matrix for understanding what his death and resurrection would be all about. The scriptures and the power of God: the ancient stories construct the world within which it makes not just sense but explosive sense to think of Jesus' crucifixion as the still point of the turning world, the moment when heaven and earth are drawn together as their Lord hangs between them, the day when the Red Sea of sin and death was defeated by God's mighty power so that all the Lord's people could pass through.

Third, a meal interpreted further through the foot-washing. Just in case anyone should imagine that what Jesus did might be of general relevance but not specifically related to them personally, Jesus comes to each in turn, comes as the Servant, comes with water and towel and washes their feet. It is an intimate, precious, private moment. And it says, as clearly as anything ever could: I'm doing this for you – yes, you, not just the person sitting next to you. And if you let me wash you, I can clean and rinse and refresh every part of you, the sad parts, the lonely parts, the messy and muddled parts, the parts you wish with all your heart could be healed. They can be. Taste my bread, drink my wine, and let me wash you. That's what my coming death is all about.

And of course among those who had their feet washed was Judah. That's the vulnerability of love, its openness to betrayal. But with that openness and danger goes something you don't get any other way. When Judah goes out into the dark, Jesus speaks of two things and two things only: glory and love. Now is the son of man glorified, and God is glorified in him. A new commandment I give you, that you love one another as I have loved you. As we take part in the ancient footwashing liturgy and consider what it means, we realize that these two things, glory and love, are not two but one. Like heaven and earth, they are joined for ever in the Servant, the son of man, the wounded, betrayed but victorious Jesus, completing the scriptures, alive with the vulnerable power of God, made known to us in the breaking of the bread.

7

GOOD FRIDAY

Behold the man! Behold your king! (John 19.1–16a)

So Pilate then took Jesus and had him flogged. The soldiers wove a crown of thorns, put it on his head, and dressed him up in a purple robe. Then they came up to him and said, 'Hail, King of the Jews!' And they slapped him.

Pilate went out again.

'Look,' he said to them, 'I'm bringing him out to you, so that you'll know I find no guilt in him.'

So Jesus came out, wearing the crown of thorns and the purple cloak.

'Look!' said Pilate. 'Here's the man!'

So when the chief priests and their attendants saw him, they gave a great shout.

'Crucify him!' they yelled. 'Crucify him!'

'Take him yourselves and crucify him!' said Pilate. 'I find him not guilty!'

'We've got a law,' replied the Judaeans, 'and according to that law he deserves to die! He made himself the son of God!'

When Pilate heard that, he was all the more afraid. He went back into the residence and spoke to Jesus.

'Where do you come from?' he asked.

But Jesus gave him no answer.

So Pilate addressed him again.

'Aren't you going to speak to me?' he said. 'Don't you know that I have the authority to let you go, and the authority to crucify you?'

'You couldn't have any authority at all over me', replied Jesus, 'unless it was given to you from above. That's why the person who handed me over to you is guilty of a greater sin.'

From that moment on, Pilate tried to let him go.

But the Judaeans shouted at him.

'If you let this fellow go,' they said, 'you are no friend of Caesar! Everyone who sets himself up as a king is speaking against Caesar!'

So when Pilate heard them saying that, he brought Jesus out and sat down at the official judgment seat, called The Pavement (in Hebrew, 'Gabbatha'). It was the Preparation day of the Passover, and it was about midday.

'Look,' said Pilate, 'here is your king!'

'Take him away!' they shouted. 'Take him away! Crucify him!'

'Do you want me to crucify your king?' asked Pilate.

'We have no king', the chief priests replied, 'except Caesar!'

Then he handed him over to them to be crucified.

The confrontation between Jesus and Pilate in John 18 and 19 is by some way the fullest account of that meeting. (It is also, incidentally, a point at which Roman historians say that we are on solid historical ground.) John has said almost nothing to this point about the Roman presence in Palestine, though the exception is highly significant. After the raising of Lazarus, Caiaphas comments that this man Jesus had better be put to death, the one rather than the many, because otherwise the Romans will come and destroy the Temple and the nation. John rubs our noses in this by referring back to it at the point of Jesus' arrest and the night hearing (18.14).

We have by now moved from Matthew to John in our journey from Palm Sunday to the foot of the cross; but it is remarkable how many of the themes converge. The link between Jesus and the Temple is strong throughout John, and it is John who dates the crucifixion of the lamb of God at the moment when the Passover lambs are being killed in the Temple. Matthew tells of the workers in the vineyard; John's Jesus is the true vine. Matthew's Jesus speaks of the messianic banquet from which one guest was excluded; John describes the supper from which Judas goes out into the night. Matthew's Jesus speaks of love as the greatest commandment; John introduces his astonishing, sustained final sequence by declaring that Jesus, having loved his own who were in the world, loved them now to the uttermost. Matthew's Jesus speaks of David's son becoming David's Lord; now Pilate says 'Behold the man', and the crowds say, 'He deserves to die, because he has claimed to be the son of God'.

And of course, running through the scene between Jesus and Pilate, with the Sadducean chief priests playing a key role, we would be deaf indeed not to hear echoes of the double debate, of the tribute-penny which declares Tiberius Caesar to be the son of God, and of the Sadducean denial of the resurrection and the revolutionary theology it embodies. Those, indeed, are front and centre in John 19. What the modern Western church has been too eager to ignore, John would not have us forget: that Jesus goes to the cross as the climax of the long story of confrontation between the creator God and the principalities and powers of the world. Jesus has already declared (18.36) that his kingdom is not *from* this world, giving as evidence the fact that his followers do not fight. But there should be no doubt that his kingdom is *for* this world, even as God's kingdom is to come *on earth* as in heaven. That is why he declares that he has come to bear witness to the truth, the truth about God's world. Equally, it is why Pilate sneers at the very notion of truth itself. The only truth he knows comes out of the scabbard of a sword. Our generation ought not to be surprised to find the question 'What is truth?' coming from a Roman governor. Postmodernity is not a new phenomenon. It's what you get when imperial violence is the only truth left standing in the playground of the philosophers.

So John, for whom Jesus' death is the ultimate act of love, the ultimate revelation of divine glory, understands that death, as do all the evangelists, in terms of the scriptures and the power of God. The Psalms, particularly 22 and 69; the prophets, particularly Isaiah and Zechariah; the Exodus narrative itself, with the lamb whose bones are not broken; all of these and more tell a single great story that is now coming to its denouement. But the story is more than the assembling of a few odd details. The large-scale scriptural story was always the account of how the one true God had called the people of Israel to be his agents, his instruments, in challenging and rolling back the power of evil which had infected the whole human race. That story itself became stuck in the problem to which it was the answer, the problem of human rebellion and sin. But from the heart of that double problem came the scriptural insistence that God would be faithful, and would send the king, the Messiah, who would complete his purpose for Israel and thereby complete his purpose for the world. That is the scriptural story, and it relies of

course on the power of the creator God to bring it
about.

Look at that story for a moment. The men of Babel
build their great tower; God confuses their language
('What is truth?' once more) and calls his servant
Abraham. Egypt enslaves God's people; God sends
Moses to confront Pharaoh and to lead the people to
freedom at Passover-time. The Philistines defeat Israel,
killing the first king, Saul; God raises up David to
establish a kingdom, promising him an heir who will
be God's own son. Babylon trumpets its pride around
the world, with Israel in shame and disgrace; now, says
YHWH, behold my servant. The imperial monsters come
up out of the sea, and God exalts the son of man as
their judge. Now read John 19 again, hear the echoes of
scripture and watch the power of God at work. Rome
does what it does best, mocking a rebel king before
brutally killing him. Pilate brings Jesus out to the
crowds, the day before Passover, and shouts, 'Behold
your king!' And the chief priests, who don't want a
Messiah any more than they want a resurrection, declare, 'We have no king but Caesar' (and if that doesn't
send a chill down your spine, you aren't awake). Here
are the powers of the world, the Babels and Egypts
and Philistines and Babylons. And here is the seed of
Abraham, the greater than Moses, the son of David, the
Servant of YHWH. Behold, the man! Behold, your king!

Of the many astonishing things in this scene, here is
one to ponder: just as John had seen Caiaphas speaking
prophetically despite himself, declaring that Jesus would
die on behalf of the people, so now he has even Pilate
speaking the truth despite his own disavowal of the
very concept. 'Here is your king!', then backed up (John

again rubs our noses in the point) with 'What I have written, I have written'. Pilate, Caesar's spokesman and hired thug, is under the authority of God despite himself. As Jesus himself says, you couldn't have any power over me unless it were given you from above. John's gospel is full of irony at every level, but this is surely the greatest: that when the empire hears the word that there is a God who might call empire to account, the empire does what it always does, mocks and kills – but that very action proves the point, because God the creator, the God of Abraham, Isaac and Jacob, does not fight the battle against evil with the weapons of the world, but with the weapons of love. As St Paul saw so clearly, Caesar's apparent victory was actually the victory of God.

And that is why, with Jesus going to his cross, God's project to heal creation itself is accomplished. John announced his intention of writing a story with that large theme in his opening words, echoing the opening of Genesis itself. In the beginning God created the heavens and the earth; now, in the beginning was the Word . . . and the Word became flesh, joining heaven and earth into one. Great themes from the creation narrative have been woven into his gospel: light and darkness, day and night, the seed which will be fruitful and multiply. Now, on the Friday, the sixth day of the week, the day of the creation of humankind in the image of God, Pilate brings Jesus out dressed in purple and wearing a crown of thorns, and declares, 'Behold the man!' And the watching world, in the persons of the chief priests and guards, shout, 'Crucify him!' When the Image of God appears in creation, the point is that the rest of creation will look at this Image and see their creator reflected. Now the son of God appears as the true Image of God, and the world is so corrupt in its rebellion that, rather than recognize the true creator God reflected in this Jesus, it must get rid of him, must blot out the reminder of who God really is, must do anything rather than be confronted by the one whose love will stop at nothing to reconcile creation to himself.

But the scriptures must be fulfilled, and the power of God will triumph. At the end of the sixth day in Genesis, God finished all his work (*synetelesen*, Genesis 2.2 LXX). At the end of the sixth day in John, Jesus declared, 'It is finished' (*tetelestai*). It is accomplished. Creation is healed. In the beginning was the Word; and the last word spoken by the living Word was the word which declared, as Jesus had in the Upper Room, 'I have finished (*teleiōsas*) the work you gave me to do' (17.4). That is, of course, how the father, the creator, is glorified. That is how love is perfected, brought to its final completion (13.1).

And we who now stand at the foot of the cross have to face the most searching questions, the questions we avoid like the plague because we, too, find it desperately uncomfortable to look at the face of God's Image, the man, the king, and see there the perfect likeness of the maker and redeemer of the world. We are so stuck in the systems of Caesar – his swords, his coins, his gambling soldiers – that we too have a hard time recognizing truth of any kind, let alone speaking up for it. We are so anxious to protect the philosophies upon which our modern world is built that we will do anything to declare that we have no king but Caesar, that when push comes to shove religion is just a private thing which mustn't affect the public sphere, even when Jesus is reminding Caesar's representative that he only has power because God has given it to him. And perhaps that is one of the reasons why the church is in such pain at the moment, caught between 'what is truth?' on the one hand and 'no king but Caesar' on the other.

But the good news – and this is after all Good Friday – is that this story, for all its searing challenge, remains the story of the scriptures and the power of God, and therefore of the glory and the love of God. John has told us all along that this will be how Jesus will reveal his glory, and here he is: Behold the man! Behold, your king! And those who pause to contemplate the Good Friday mystery, to reflect, ponder and to pray, will come above all to discover that when we look at the face of the crucified Jesus we are looking into the face of the God who loved the world so much that he gave his only son, not to condemn but to save. The good shepherd has loved his own sheep and has given his life for them. No one has greater love than this, to lay down one's life for one's friends. Jesus, having loved his own who were in the world, loved them to the uttermost. This is the love which shines out at the very moment when the darkness seemed after all to have overcome the light.

And this is the love upon which we stake our lives, our loves, our hopes. We come to Good Friday like beggars to a banquet, starved of love and suddenly finding more than we can cope with. And if it is true that that love must transform our whole lives, our public life, our grasp on truth on the one hand, our dealings with Caesar on the other, this can only be if we are first grasped and transformed by that same love at the very deepest level of our own personalities. We are invited to stand with Mary and John at the foot of the cross, at the point where heaven and earth meet, so that the love from heaven can embrace us, creatures of earth that we are; so that the light of heaven can heal the darkness within us and within the world; so that, by the power of the creator God and in accordance with the scriptures, we can ourselves become part of that new creation which for the moment, for the still, sad sabbath rest, lies waiting, buried, within the womb of the old.

8
EASTER VIGIL

Come and see! Go and tell!
(Matthew 28.1–10)

———◆———

Dawn was breaking on the first day of the week; the sabbath was over. Mary Magdalene, and the other Mary, had come to look at the tomb, when suddenly there was a great earthquake. An angel of the Lord came down from heaven. He came to the stone, rolled it away, and sat down on top of it. Looking at him was like looking at lightning, and his clothes were white, like snow. The guards trembled with terror at him, and became like corpses themselves.

'Don't be afraid,' said the angel to the women. 'I know you're looking for Jesus, who was crucified. He isn't here! He's been raised, as he said he would be! Come and see the place where he was lying – and then go at once, and tell his disciples that he's been raised from the dead, and that he's going on ahead of you to Galilee. That's where you'll see him. There: I've told you.'

The women scurried off quickly, away from the tomb, in a mixture of terror and great delight, and went to tell his disciples. Suddenly, there was Jesus himself. He met them and said, 'Greetings!' They came up to him and took hold of his feet, prostrating themselves in front of him.

'Don't be afraid,' said Jesus to them. 'Go and tell my brothers that I'm going off to Galilee. Tell them they'll see me there.'

If you asked people out on the street, or even perhaps in church, which is the most frequently repeated commandment in the Bible, the answers you'd get would probably be in the range of 'Don't misbehave', 'Don't tell lies', 'Always say your prayers', and perhaps 'Love God and your neighbour'.

But all of them would be wrong. Far and away the most frequent commandment in the Bible is what the angel says to the women, and what Jesus then repeats: 'Don't be afraid.' Yes, something new has happened. Yes, the world is never going to be the same again. Yes, your life is about to be turned upside down and inside out. Yes, God is going to be with you and demand new things of you. But *don't be afraid*. It's going to be all right. Easter proves it. That is the first great emphasis of Matthew's account of the first Easter morning.

Of course, they had every reason to be afraid. An earthquake; an angel; the guards struck down as though they were dead. We tend to think of things like that as interventions within our natural order, but that's not how they appear in the light of Easter. We have been contemplating, during the course of this book, the way in which Matthew's gospel leads us from Palm Sunday to Good Friday. Matthew shows us how, as Jesus goes to the cross, heaven and earth, God's space and our space, are drawn together in a new way. The events that are unfolding carry cosmic significance. Jesus has gone to his death bearing the weight of evil, the evil that has infected and corrupted human life and the whole world, the evil which is symbolized both by what we call human evil, not least the evil of arrogant human empire, and by what we call natural evil, the waves and storms of the physical world. Now here, with the defeat of evil and death in the cross, the earthquake and the angel are, strangely, just what we ought to expect. And the guards, symbolizing here the political and military powers for whom they are working, are struck dumb. Pilate, Herod and Caiaphas and their henchmen don't belong in this new world, the new world where heaven and earth have come rushing together in a fresh way, a fresh celebration, a world full of new possibilities, new power which leaves the powers of the world lying helpless on the ground. Don't be afraid! God's new world has begun, and you're invited to be part of it. That is what Easter is all about. That is what baptism and confirmation are all about.

The invitation takes two forms, here in Matthew's Easter gospel. First, 'Come and see'; second, 'Go and tell'.

'Come and see.' When the Christian gospel bursts upon your consciousness, all kinds of questions come up. Can it really be true? Might it not all be imagination, or even wishful thinking? Well, come and see. Actually, anything less like wishful thinking it would be hard to imagine. When I'm half awake, what I wish for is that I could go back to sleep, not that someone would grab me by the shoulder and yank me out of bed, blinking into the morning light – an image that may be too close for comfort for some people attending an early morning Easter Vigil. But that's what Easter is all about. God's new world has broken in to the old one, putting the clocks forward so that the morning has come before we're really ready for it. No, this isn't wishful thinking. It's reality.

But recognizing the new reality is just the beginning of obeying the command to 'come and see'. Come with your questions. Come and examine the evidence, the evidence about Jesus' life and death, the evidence –

which is wonderfully strong – about his bodily resurrection. The path ahead of you may look misty, but as you start to walk on it you'll find it's rock solid. Come and see for yourself what it means to live on the basis that two thousand years ago something happened by which death itself was defeated, that God's power was unleashed in accordance with the great stories and promises of scripture, that new creation began with a bang and that nothing has been the same since.

And of course the Easter invitation to come and see involves walking right past the sleeping guards. We have learned to be afraid of them: the outward forces that sneer at us, in public life, at school, in the media, maybe even at home; the inward voices that say you can't live like that, you can't actually live as though you were dead to sin and alive to God, as Paul says you are once you're baptized, the secret whispers that say you know sin will trip you up again so you might as well give in at once. It is indeed possible for Christians to forget the angel's command not to be afraid, and to allow the very sight of these guards to put us off from coming to the tomb and seeing for ourselves, from looking long and hard at the fact that sin and death really are beaten enemies and that we can safely ignore the soldiers from now on. Don't be afraid. Once you have come through the waters of baptism they have no rights over you; and they will only have power over you if you let them. That is why Paul insists that you must reckon, calculate, work it out, that because of your baptism you are truly dead to sin and alive to God in the Messiah, Jesus. Come and see. Work it out. Walk right past the guards and don't be afraid.

But as soon as you come and see there is the third Easter command: don't be afraid, come and see, and then 'Go and tell'. At the heart of the mystery of God's new creation is the strange truth that it happens, it spreads, when people tell others about it. From the very beginning of the coming together of heaven and earth in a new way, of the fact that knowing things in God's new world is always an act of *love* – from the very beginning, God's new creation happens when people tell others that Jesus has been raised from the dead. God wants new creation to happen *through* his renewed people, because new creation is all about trust, all about new relationships, all about love. It isn't as though the new creation were a great machine rumbling into action. It is precisely a new *creation*, and as with the first creation we humans are called to play an active role within its developing life. Go and tell and watch it happen! That's why we greet one another with the Easter greeting: Christ is risen; risen indeed, Alleluia! With that greeting, that telling, *God's new world happens*, comes into being.

Ah, you may say, all that 'telling' business, that's for the professionals. Not true. Notice who are the first, the very first, to be told to go and tell. Not the big strong leaders. Not Peter and the Twelve. They are away, hiding, afraid. It is the unlikely people, the women – in that culture, the insignificant and untrustworthy ones! – who are given the ultimate trust, who are the first to see and hear and touch the risen Jesus. He repeats the angel's command: don't be afraid, *go and tell*. This is quite deliberate. Two or three frightened women won't convince anyone by their own persuasiveness. The message will do its work through them. Go and tell! If they can, you can.

That's why confirmation means what it means; that, indeed, is why Easter is such an excellent time for it to happen. All the baptized are commanded to go and tell, but we can only ever obey if God's spirit works through us and in us. In confirmation the church prays for that spirit to come afresh upon the candidates – not that the spirit has not been at work already in their lives, because otherwise they wouldn't have come this far, but that as a church we pray together that God's spirit will indwell them in new ways as members of the body of Christ. Confirmation is a kind of lay ordination, a commissioning in the power of the spirit to become an agent of God's new creation, an Easter morning person, someone who comes to see and goes to tell and who is learning not to be afraid.

That is why Easter is the ultimate right moment to baptize and confirm. That is why, in many traditions, Christians renew their baptismal vows on Easter morning. That is why the whole church is invited again to come and see, and recommissioned again to go and tell. And that is why we are commanded, gloriously, not to be afraid. Jesus Christ is risen from the dead; God's new creation has begun; and you are summoned to be part of that, part of the new world in which earth and heaven have become one, and a new knowing, the knowing of love, is brought to birth to witness it. The scriptures and the power of God are now yours, your strength, your energy, your comfort, your guide; because they point to Jesus, the Jesus who died and is alive for evermore and who meets you on Easter morning with greeting and commissioning. Come and see; go and tell; and don't be afraid.

Alleluia! Christ is risen!
He is risen indeed, Alleluia!

9
EASTER MORNING

New temple, new creation
(John 20.1–10)

On the first day of the week, very early, Mary Magdalene came to the tomb while it was still dark.

She saw that the stone had been rolled away from the tomb. So she ran off, and went to Simon Peter, and to the other disciple, the one Jesus loved.

'They've taken the Master out of the tomb!' she said. 'We don't know where they've put him!'

So Peter and the other disciple set off and came to the tomb. Both of them ran together. The other disciple ran faster than Peter, and got to the tomb first. He stooped down and saw the linen cloths lying there, but he didn't go in. Then Simon Peter came up, following him, and went into the tomb. He saw the linen cloths lying there, and the napkin that had been around his head, not lying with the other cloths, but folded up in a place by itself.

Then the other disciple, who had arrived first at the tomb, went into the tomb as well. He saw, and he believed. They did not yet know, you see, that the Bible had said he must rise again from the dead.

Then the disciples returned to their homes.

'He saw, and believed; for as yet they did not understand the scripture, that he must rise again from the dead.' That comment from the evangelist provides a powerful link right back through John's gospel. His Easter story is not just a strange event tacked on the

76

end; it's the point towards which the entire drama has been moving.

Throughout Holy Week we have been thinking about the way in which the events of Palm Sunday lead us inexorably forwards to the cross and resurrection, through the stories and themes which the evangelists place at this point. There's a puzzle here, because in John's gospel the so-called 'cleansing of the Temple', which we associate with Palm Sunday, takes place at the start of Jesus' public career, not right at its end. But the words Jesus says there echo through the whole gospel as a major theme which finds full resolution on Easter Day itself. 'Destroy this Temple', says Jesus, 'and in three days I will build it up.' Jesus' hearers misunderstand him; but John comments that he was speaking of the 'temple' of his body. So, John adds, when he was raised from the dead, they remembered what he had said, and they believed the scripture and the word that Jesus had spoken.

For John, then, Easter is the rebuilding of the Temple, the place where God's sphere and ours intersect, where God meets with his people in grace and mercy and delight. When we say, 'Alleluia, Christ is risen', we are not saying 'Something very strange has just happened which provides a happy ending after all the sorrow of Holy Week and Good Friday', we are saying that the dwelling place of God is with humans, that he has come to be with us, and made us his people, and that God will wipe away all tears from all eyes. He begins that process in the next paragraph of John's Easter story, meeting Mary Magdalene as she stands weeping outside the tomb.

But in this first paragraph there is something very strange going on. People in the gospel story do not normally run. Let alone do they race against one another. Yet here everyone is running: Mary dashing to tell the disciples about the empty tomb, Peter and the beloved disciple running back, John getting there first, Peter catching him up and blundering ahead into the tomb, John following him in, seeing and believing. Breathless eyewitness testimony; and also the signs of something so shocking, so unexpected, so cataclysmic that the only proper response is indeed breathless haste, to find out what's going on, to discover what it all means.

If there is a biblical backdrop to the race to the tomb, it might be the two men in 2 Samuel 18, running to bring King David news of the victory over Absalom and his rebellion. The first one arrives and announces a great victory; the second one arrives and declares that the rebel leader himself is dead. The news was of course bittersweet for David; 'Would God I had died for you,' he says, 'O Absalom, my son, my son.' But now, kaleidoscopically, the news for which Peter and John have raced to the tomb goes out into all the world; great David's greater son has indeed given his life for his rebel subjects; David's Lord, the only son of the father, has defeated the ultimate enemy, death itself and the sin which causes it. He has won the messianic victory over all the forces of chaos and destruction.

And that is why the second great theme of John's Easter story, alongside the new Temple, is the new creation. We saw on Good Friday how on that day, the sixth day of the week, the day when human beings were created in God's image to rule as stewards over creation, Pilate brings Jesus out to the crowds and declares,

'Behold the man!' And Jesus goes to his death with the final word *tetelestai*, it is accomplished. It is complete. Like God himself on the evening of the sixth day of the week, he has finished the work, the great task. He has then spent the long sabbath at rest:

> O Sabbath rest by Calvary,
> O calm of tomb below,
> Where the grave-clothes and the spices
> Cradle him we did not know.
> Rest you well, beloved Jesus,
> Caesar's Lord and Israel's King,
> In the brooding of the Spirit
> In the darkness of the spring.

But now it is the first day of the week; the day after the sabbath, the eighth day, the start of God's new world. It is early morning, still dark. It is the moment of new creation, the moment towards which John's gospel has been moving ever since his reimagining of creation itself in his Prologue; in him was life, and the life was the light of human beings; the light shines in the darkness, and the darkness has not overcome it. Mary Magdalene doesn't know this yet; she comes to the tomb while it is still dark, only to be confronted with the initial evidence that the son of God has risen, a truth so bright that she can't yet look at it. When we see her again, in the next paragraph, the echoes of Genesis are unmistakable: she imagines Jesus to be the gardener. The whole scene declares, through symbol and echo and the onrush of themes from the whole gospel story: new creation has begun, and you're invited to be part of it!

That is, in fact, the central message of Easter Day, though the Western church has been quick to downgrade it in favour of something else. Easter is not the proof of life after death. Easter is not even primarily the proof that there is a life *after* 'life after death', a new bodily life after a period of being physically dead. Of course, if people don't believe those things, Easter is multiple good news; but the point is not that Easter is there to teach us a general truth, but that Easter is itself the *beginning of* that 'life after life after death', that after-afterlife, the bursting in of the new creation upon a surprised and unready world, a new creation which is every bit as physical as you and me and indeed much more so, since this new body, Jesus' risen body, the prototype of new creation, is alive with a life which can't be harmed, cannot be touched by corruption or death.

This is a shock and a scandal – and it's the best news there ever was. It demands that we rethink our world-views and reorder our priorities and re-tell our controlling stories with this new Fact in the middle, a fact which calls into question our cheap little notions of what 'facts' themselves really are. Easter is about something that's happened, not about ideas in people's heads or even faith in their hearts. God's new creation has begun; the kingdom of God has appeared on earth as it is in heaven; and you're invited to be part of it, to be plunged into it in baptism, to eat and drink it in the Eucharist, to celebrate it in worship and to explore it in prayer.

And – to make it happen in the world. That is the primary calling of Easter, and Christian spirituality at its most authentic is about sustaining and equipping us for that task. Easter is not telling us that there is after all an escape hatch from the world, a private ladder up to a disembodied heaven. This is where so many of the Easter hymns, including alas some of my own favourites, get it wrong, or at least only half right, and the wrong half at that. Easter is not about the fact that 'Heaven's bright gates are open held', though they are; it's about the fact that the powerful new life of heaven has come to birth on the earth, and that we are to be its agents as well as its beneficiaries. Easter is not the celebration that Jesus is king 'above the sky', as though he'd simply, as we say, 'died and gone to heaven'. Easter is the celebration that he is Lord of earth as well as heaven. The message he 'bids us tell abroad' is not simply about 'how we too may enter heaven'; it's about how we can make new creation happen here and now. I suspect that at least half the reason why an older liberal theology felt obliged to oppose the orthodox view of Easter was because for the last two centuries, in our conniving at the Platonism of the Enlightenment, the church has said 'Christ is risen' and has meant 'so there is a supernatural world after all into which we can escape, with Jesus leading the way'. That wasn't and isn't the message of Easter.

The message is that new creation has begun, and you are called to belong to it and to make it happen in the world – whether by campaigning for making poverty history, for peace and justice in the Middle East, for a new start for refugees and asylum-seekers, or for a fresh vision of where we should be going in our country, in Europe, in our schools and hospitals and cities and villages. Take the scriptures in one hand and the power of God in the other, take a deep breath of the air of new creation which blows through the world on Easter Day, and find what *you* can do to make new creation happen. The powers of death and hell will be cross with you for doing so, and you'll face battles on the way. Go back again and again to the fact of Easter; the enemies are a beaten rabble, God's new creation will win the day, and you must be part of it. That is why the Easter message is a message of love, the love which believes the resurrection itself, the love which reaches up to God in gratitude and out to the world in generosity.

One of the key places to begin is with your own self. Our grand visions of God's new world can sometimes draw attention away from the personal battles with evil. We are sometimes tempted to think, 'If I work hard at bringing new creation to the world, I won't have to focus on how I behave, my own habits and choices and style of life.' Well, you will. If you want to be an Easter person for God's world, an agent of new creation, you can't refuse the challenge of Colossians 3, the traditional Easter morning epistle.

In Colossians 3.1–11, Paul talks very straight about what living as Easter people looks like in practice. He lists a lot of rubbish from the old creation which must be left behind in the tomb; five kinds of sexual immorality, five kinds of angry talk and behaviour. All of these are kinds of untruth, ways of behaving and speaking which are out of line with God's good creation. If the church had grasped Colossians 3 we wouldn't be in the mess we're in. Instead, he says – echoing the baptismal imagery which has been associated with Easter from earliest times – you have stripped off the old clothing, the old self with its lifestyle, and have put on the new clothes, the new self which is being renewed in knowledge according to the image of the creator. Easter is good news for the world; but it's got to start at home.

Our Holy Week journey is complete; and yet it is not complete. Easter is a beginning, not an ending. None of the four gospels ends its Easter account with a sense of 'Well, that's all right then; the story's over, we can breathe a sigh of relief.' Each of them, in their four very different ways, says something much more like: 'Now that the great battle has been won, you have a job to do. There's a world out there, God's Spirit will give you the energy and direction, and you are called to be renewed humans for the sake of God's new world.'

I am reminded of the story – I've heard it told of various people – about the professor who was in the middle of a lecture when it was announced that war had broken out and things had to stop. Six years later he went into the same classroom and began, 'As I was saying when I was so rudely interrupted . . .'. That is a bit what Easter is like. Now that the battle is won, now that sin has been defeated, let's get on with being real, genuine human beings. Now that death itself has been overcome, let's get on with the real human task, of bringing God's new life to his whole world.

One of the great Easter hymns catches this brilliantly:

Now let the heavens be joyful,
And earth her song begin;
The round world keep high triumph,
And *all* that is therein.

Yes. The heavens are indeed joyful; it's our job to get earth to join in the song. Christ the Lord hath risen, our joy that hath no end; yes, indeed, and it's about time the round world shared that high triumph, and all that is therein. We're the Easter people; let's get on with it.